moon chimes

poems

Laura L. B. Border

Laurelle Communications
Boulder, Colorado

Laurelle Communications
285 Devon Place
Boulder, Colorado 80302-8033
LaurelleCommunications.com

Copyright © 2021 by Laura L. B. Border

All rights reserved. No part of this book may be reproduced or used in any manner whatsoever without the written permission of the publisher, except for brief quotations included in critical articles and reviews.

Printed in the United States of America

Book and cover design by Sandra Jonas

ISBN: 978-1-9541100-0-7

*To my daughter, Alison,
who relished my project*

Contents

Acknowledgments vii

Introduction ix

Butter Moon 1

Button Moon 3

Mulligatawny Moon 4

A Full Moon Duet 5

Cat and Mouse Moon 6

June Moon 7

City Moon 8

Moonlight on Flagstaff 9

Harvest Moon 10

Hermit Moon 11

White on White 12

Christmas Moon 13

The Blue Moon Ballet 14

Rocky Mountain Moons   15

Supermoon at Dusk   16

Sky's Eye Moon   18

Marigold Moon   19

About the Author   21

For Further Reading 22

Acknowledgments

In school I learned to "do my own work." As a writer, I have learned how much I benefit from the input of talented readers. *Moon Chimes* sat on my shelf for years. Then a friend read it and suggested publication. I worked on the poems and put them back on my shelf. Then this year, a local writers' contest had a poetry section. I decided to enter because the judges were expected to give written feedback on the work entered. I submitted three poems, all of which received positive feedback.

Soon after, I mentioned the contest to another writer friend, and she volunteered to read the whole collection and give me feedback. Unbeknownst to me, she had assisted other writers with their works of poetry. With delight, I sent the poems and the feedback from the contest off to her. She returned the poems with beneficial suggestions, corrections, and heartfelt encouragement. A month later, she mentioned that she kept remembering the images from my poems. Her feedback inspired me to re-edit and publish this collection.

I extend my deepest gratitude to Avery Russell, a superb and artistic editor who asks the right questions and identifies the gaps and mistakes; Julie Schneider, whose clear scientific mind makes me put things in order while her sense of humor and loving heart lift me up; my daughter, Alison Border Rakotonirina, whose creative energy is inspirational and whose reading and editing skills hone the big meanings and catch the tiny typos; and Bill Border, a fine art painter and my husband, whose pointers on aesthetics always lead to balance and beauty.

Finally, I am grateful to Sandra Jonas and her team at Sandra Jonas Publishing House for their enthusiasm, expertise, and guidance in producing this volume of poems.

Introduction

In 1991, I decided to observe the full moon each month as inspiration for my writing. My goal was to write poems that captured my experience. *Moon Chimes* is the result of my study. Although one month I was sick in bed and had to write a poem about the moon shining through my bedroom window, the remaining poems are my interpretation of how the moon appeared in the sky on each particular occurrence. That year boasted a blue moon in December as well, resulting in a total of thirteen tributes to the full moon. I added a summary poem to close the collection.

    The project was instructive. I have always loved seeing the full moon rise over the eastern horizon, but I had never paid much attention to its monthly variations. Each month I was surprised by the changes in the aspects of the moon depending on the weather, the humidity, the clarity or fogginess of the atmosphere, the time of the year, the exact time of moonrise, or the degree at which it rose on the horizon. Searching for inspiration in a deliberate way at a certain time of each month has expanded my awareness of astronomy, my vocabulary, and my creativity.

Having one theme—the full moon—but various interpretations of it has forced me to develop different metaphors for the same subject. My response to the visual impact of the moon in the night sky engendered images that coalesced into varied visual descriptions and effects.

Over the last few years, I have joyfully gone out to observe supermoons. Supermoons appear exceptionally large because they occur at the perigee when the moon is closest to the earth. Three poems about the spring 2020 supermoons follow the original 1991 poems.

The moon has been the muse of poets for centuries. One of my favorite moon poems is Arthur Rimbaud's "La lune comme un point sur un i"—that is, "The Moon Like a Dot on an I." *Moon Chimes* is my contribution to the ongoing dialogue. I hope my poems will encourage you to watch the moon more closely and to craft your own responses to her phases.

Butter Moon
(January)

From my perch on a rocky hill, I gaze eastward at a winter landscape reduced to its starkest form.

Before me, I see a picture cut perfectly into thirds:

> The top of the canvas is lightly brushed
> with hues of gray.
>
> Rectangular barns and houses float
> on windswept islands of smooth snow.
>
> Lavender shadows paint map shapes
> around honey-colored grasses, nestling below
> the feathery tips of winter's bare branches.

I gasp as the moon pops up over the horizon—a bright yellow disk, an impossible butter moon, dripping languid golden beams through the misty evening light.

I watch as her rays of light flood over the organic shapes of darkened pines. Shafts of yellow flow over low-lying junipers—cascading from bush to bush, they illuminate shadowed nooks.

I glance behind me—
    the sleepy sun drops out of sight
    behind rugged western peaks.

Turning my eyes to the east once more,
    I observe the moon's otherworldliness soaring
    higher and higher,
        flaunting the legerdemain of the universe.

Button Moon
(February)

A drifting milky way of clouds hangs like a scarf
    against the dark round shoulders of the night.

On the flowing cloak of darkness, the moon dangles
    like a button tugging to be set free.

She is trapped, as I am, between winter and spring,
    desiring the lightness of a warm summer breeze.

But the reluctant sky embraces winter,
    drawing the heavenly fabric stitched with star
    threads even closer still.

Mulligatawny Moon
(March)

Tonight, I couldn't see the moon—
a dark drifting mass of heavy clouds separated us.

When the moon squinted through like a myopic eye,
I looked up in despair at the disappointing sight.

How could I write a full moon poem when her
beauty malingered?

Nonetheless I'll try . . .

    Not magnificent, but muddled and murky,
      the moon mopes behind a mulligatawny mist.

    A mournful martyr, miserable and maudlin,
        I pout—mad as a March Hare—
    because my earthbound view prevents me from seeing
        the moon's magical merriment.

A Full Moon Duet
(April)

Shafts of moonlight pour through the shutters,
casting moon shadows on the bed where I lie enfevered.

Bathed in moonlight I recline,
my full cleavage bursting against soft folds of gown.

My pale skin reflects the caressing light.

As the moonlight forms the opposite of shadows,
round dark phantoms drape my hips—
shadows enfolding the light.

Cat and Mouse Moon
(May)

From my porch I expected to see the moon high in
 the clear northern sky.
The moon was absent.
Only faint stars traced constellations in the heavens.

I walked farther into the garden.
Like a cat I crept around the rose bush
Expecting to pounce on at least a yellow moonbeam.

A faint glimmer shining through the foliage caught
 my eye.
I took one more step and looked upward toward the
 southern horizon.
Astonished, I pondered my ignorance of patterns—
 the branches above me cradled the grinning face
 of the moon.

June Moon
(June)

I awake early in the morning to observe the full moon.
Low in the western sky,
    June Moon cruises over the mountains.
Her cold regolith-covered surface reflects the ghost-
    like earthshine.

Fifteen days before a full solar eclipse,
    Lady Moon, star of the night, is planning
    a daytime performance.
Traveling along her ellipsis, she journeys toward
    her moment of power.
For seven full minutes the moon will eclipse
    the burning, broiling, exploding source of
    her earth-faced reflection.

City Moon
(July)

To the east, the city sprawls
beneath the lemon light of the summer moon.

City lights mimic the moon's papery glow—
red lights, green lights,
streetlights, headlights—
a warm holiday scene.

Aloft, mellow and serene—
Japanese lanternesque—
the moon's full roundness brushes against the night.

Moonlight on Flagstaff
(August)

Overhead the marbled white moon teases.
On earth, dark mountain shapes jut jauntily
into the depths of nightfall.
Footsteps behind me rustle as shiny sneakers
jump from rock to rock.

Couples in white shirts sit spaced out
on the boulders below me.
With their faces upturned, their whispers echo—
floating and bouncing—off the steep cliffs.
Watching their warm bodies embrace in the cool air,
I face the void, wrapped in moonlight.

Harvest Moon
(September)

The golden round Harvest Moon marks the end
    and the beginning.
Tenacious leaves still cushion the evening sky,
While their crackling sisters skitter here and there
    on earth.

Brittle breezes envelope me.
Invisible fingers slide up my spine chilling me
    to the bone.
I shiver and remember a colder season yet to come.

Encased in a heavy woolen sweater and scarf—
    like the bounty held in round, red, yellow,
    orange, green, and purple mounds of vegetable
    flesh—
I yearn for the naked extravagance of spring.

Hermit Moon
(October)

Above me a white circle Moon
cuts a hole in the black canopy of night.

As I walk on Enchanted Mesa,
the moon lights my way.

Fallen pine needles muffle the sound of my footsteps.

Alone in the darkness, I sense
the almost imperceptible transformation
of earth, moon, and planets—
suspended and turning.

White on White
(November)

A sailing moon speeds across the pale evening sky.
Wisps of clouds filter bands of moonlight
onto the slushy streets below.

The moon's inorganic light,
piercing newly bared branches,
reflects off the snow-covered rooftops
of the neighborhood.

I open my eyes wide to follow her otherworldly
movement.
My ears fill with the sound of water
dripping from the gutters.

My skin shivers in the chilly fall air.
The hairs in my nose tickle with the clarity of the season,
as spinning, the moon and I rush into winter.

Christmas Moon
(December)

As I await moonrise from high on Enchanted Mesa,
Whiffs of wood smoke hang in the still air.
The cold pricks my face as puffs of my breath
waft off like ghosts.
I watch the horizon closely.

In the blink of an eye, the actress explodes onto stage.
La Lune
La Luna
Christmas Moon

Her stark red beauty floods the sky.
Stars flicker and go out.
Constellations disappear.
Galaxies fade in lunar light.
Faint moon shadows kiss the snow.

And I, caught in communion with the Goddess,
drink in the blood of the moment—
illusion and reality are one.

The Blue Moon Ballet
(December)

Blue Moon
Rare Moon
Filmy veils spin softly o'er you,
rainbow circles bend round your brow,
their luminous blues, reds, and golds
light up the darkness.

Blue Moon
Dancing Moon
Behind you, your sister stars twinkle,
tiny Belles decorating the heavens.
Tinkling, the stars turn pirouettes on pointed toes.

Blue Moon
Thirteenth Moon
You are the Star tonight, the prima ballerina
of this nighttime show.
As I watch, the corps de ballet glides into the wings,
offering you center stage for your moonlight
extravaganza.

Rocky Mountain Moons
(December 1991)

One Moon—
Thirteen whole notes with
variations on a theme.
Moon mountain melodies:

Presto—
Winter moon scoots rapidly behind frigid veils.

Adagio—
Spring moon opens leisurely drooping petals of light
to kiss the hilltops.

Andante—
Summer moon rises languidly above the southern horizon.

Vivace—
Autumn moon scuttles as witches cackle.

Supermoon at Dusk
(Full Supermoon March 2020)

Above a narrow ribbon of blue, white layers of clouds veil the evening sky.

As I watch from my perch at an elevation of 5700 feet, bright red taillights create a red ribbon rising south along the turnpike on Davidson Mesa.

Along South Boulder Road to the east, headlights drop into Boulder Valley forming a luminescent yellow snake.

At exactly 7:12 MDT a short bright orange line appears on the horizon at 83 degrees.

Within seconds the orange line transforms into a glowing arc—a surprising pumpkin-top moon appearing in the month of March.

After a minute has gone by, the pumpkin flattens as it rises behind the horizontal layer of clouds.

Soon it appears to be a horizontal orange cylinder
    caught between the cloudbank's edge and
    the earth's horizon.

Slowly the squashed pumpkin floats upward to
    disappear behind the clouds where its
    reflected light cannot pierce the cloudy haze.

In my mind's eye, I imagine the Supermoon in its
    full glory—reflecting sunlight back to watchers
    somewhere on earth.

Sky's Eye Moon
(Full Supermoon April 7, 2020)

Posed alone in the sky
unfettered by cloud forms
so bright the stars were hidden,
the moon appeared to be a bright hole
at the base of a cone formed by the firmament.

My senses turned topsy-turvy as I gazed into it,
fearing that I might fall in.

Marigold Moon
(Full Supermoon May 2020)

The sky was dark.
The foothills surrounding me were pitch black.
Tucked warmly in my Honda CRV, I awaited
    the rise of the third supermoon of 2020.

Expecting the moon to rise due east from my perch
    on the hill above Boulder,
I was surprised by its late arrival.

As I glanced southward, the yellow stream
    of headlights dropping into the Boulder Valley
    drew my attention.
A round glowing arc was rising just above
    the yellow ribbon of light.

"There it is!" I shrieked. "The moon is so far south
    tonight."

I watched in wonder as the glorious golden full
    supermoon rose higher in the sky—a celestial
    marigold blossom mocking the tiny electric
    car lamps below.

About the Author

Laura L. B. Border's love of literature began when she was a small child. She memorized long poems and recited them to her little brothers at bedtime. Her love of nature was internalized at the age of six when she began riding her pony, Mickey, around the Yampa Valley. In college, she studied languages and literatures—French, English, German, Spanish, and Romance Linguistics.

As an instructor of French language and literature at the University of Colorado, Boulder, she coauthored the successful *Collage* and *Montage* French college textbooks for McGraw-Hill. Later in her career, she directed the Graduate Teacher Program and published in a variety of educational journals. Currently, she devotes her time to writing and gardening at her home in Boulder, Colorado.

For Further Reading

Follow Laura L. B. Border on Instagram: @laurewest.

Laura writes a monthly blog on writing novels, posted on the seventh day of the month: laurellecommunications.com.

If you're interested in using *Moon Chimes* in a classroom or homeschooling environment, the *Moon Chimes Workbook* will be published in 2021. The workbook combines the arts and sciences to help students learn more about astronomy and explore their own creativity.

This book is set in Sabon, designed by the accomplished typographer Jan Tschichold (1902–1974) and released in 1967. The font is based on the work of Claude Garamond (1480–1561), a famous Parisian publisher and one of the most influential typographers of all time. Tschichold named his creation after Jacques Sabon, one of Garamond's students. Today, Sabon is the official typeface for the prestigious Stanford University.

www.ingramcontent.com/pod-product-compliance
Lightning Source LLC
Chambersburg PA
CBHW031508040426
42444CB00007B/1263